"LISTE DES FRANÇOIS ET SUISSES"

FROM AN OLD MANUSCRIPT LIST OF

FRENCH AND SWISS PROTESTANTS

SETTLED IN

CHARLESTON, ON THE SANTEE

AND AT THE

ORANGE QUARTER

IN CAROLINA

WHO DESIRED NATURALIZATION

PREPARED PROBABLY ABOUT 1695–6

CLEARFIELD COMPANY
REPRINTS & REMAINDERS

Originally Published
Charleston, 1868

Republished
New York, 1888

Reprinted
Genealogical Publishing Company
Baltimore, 1968

Reprinted for Clearfield Company Inc. by
Genealogical Publishing Co. Inc.
Baltimore, MD 1990

Library of Congress Catalog Card Number 68-22956

Reprinted from a copy
loaned to us by
The South Carolinian Library,
University of South Carolina,
Columbia, South Carolina

CONTENTS.

INTRODUCTION.

A short time ago I published two pamphlets under the title of "A Contribution to the History of the Huguenots of South Carolina." Since that time, that to which these lines act as an introduction was sent to me by my kinsman, Dr. F. Peyre Porcher, of Charleston, S. C., with a note saying that he had received it from its compiler, Mr. Daniel Ravenel. It appears to me to possess sufficient interest to warrant its publication, and I have had it reproduced in a style conformable with the previous issue, in order that they may be bound together. It will be noticed that all the inaccuracies of grammar and orthography and all the inelegancies of diction which characterized the original pamphlet have been preserved in this.

THEODORE GAILLARD THOMAS, M.D.

NEW YORK, Feb. 28, 1888.

PREFATORY NOTE.

The articles, of which this pamphlet is a republication, were contributed by me in June, 1822, to the *Southern Intelligencer*, a religious paper, then issued weekly in Charleston. The object was to furnish the descendants of the French and Swiss Refugees, in print, the contents of an old manuscript List of Refugees, in the possession of our family. Of this manuscript, therefore, some account is given in No. 4 of the Articles. To what is there said I may add that it was found among sundry old papers, most of them of little or no value, at the plantation known as *Wantoot*, in St. John's, Berkley, which had been the residence of my father and grandfather. It is not a general list of the Refugees ; it purports to be a list of such as desired an Act of Naturalization. Its character was found to give it an interest beyond the purpose for which it was designed. To the names of persons on the list are added their places of nativity, their parentage, the persons they married, the children born before, and those born after, their arrival in Carolina ; and the mothers and wives are, with few exceptions, mentioned by their maiden names. This last feature is in accordance with the rights of married persons under the Civil Law, which is the basis of the French Code. Under the English Common Law " Husband and Wife are one person " and their legal rights are modified by this principle. " In the Civil Law the husband and wife are considered two distinct persons, and may have different estates, etc." [1] The preservation of the born names of women thus has importance in France. To us the interest of the paper consists chiefly in the genealogies it records.

The manuscript is in my possession ; and although mutilated by age, will be cheerfully submitted to the inspection of persons interested in the genealogies.

The manuscript occupies seventeen pages of fool's-cap paper. The first part paged from 1 to 13, the remainder not paged.

The portions are

    1. The principal List, numbered from 1 to 119 inclusive, which is the list published in 1822.

    2. The portion marked ☞ No. 2, purporting to be names of persons at Orange Quarter, which, from the note at its close was imperfect and collected in aid of a committee.

---

[1] 1 Blackstone Comment., ch. 15.

3. The portion marked ☞ No. 3, which has
been, and is now, supposed to consist of
notes used in the compiling the principal
list ; and this formed the envelope of all
the sheets and is endorsed "*List des François et Suisses.*"

For the reasons stated, Nos. 2 and 3 were not
published in 1822 : it is now deemed advisable to
print them also.

The writing of these last is read with difficulty,
and I am indebted for aid in making these tran-
scripts, to the kindness of Mr. LOUIS MANIGAULT,
of this city, whose familiarity with old French chi-
rography has enabled me to present them.

Soon after the original publication Mr. HENRY
H. BACOT, of this city, visited France and became
acquainted with the BACOT family, residing a few
miles from Tours. He had with him the *Southern Intelligencer* containing this list. The identity
of the families was recognized ; and the Baron BACOT
DE ROMAINE extended many kindnesses to his re-
mote relative, and also accorded civilities to others
from South Carolina. In consequence of this
pleasant result, the late venerable THOMAS WRIGHT
BACOT, brother of Mr. H. H. BACOT (remembered by
many as the first Postmaster of Charleston under
the Federal Government), caused the articles to
be republished in the *City Gazette* in May, 1826.

I have been unable to find a copy of the original

publication in the *Southern Intelligencer* or even
to ascertain if its files have been preserved. The
present publication is made from a volume of the
City Gazette in the Treasury Office of Charleston, kindly lent me for the purpose by the Hon. P.
C. GAILLARD, Mayor.

The spelling, both of names and words in this
List, is not uniform. Some names we know from
other documents to be erroneously written, for in-
stance " MANIGAUD " for " MANIGAULT," " GOUR-
DAIN " for " GOURDIN," but, as the purpose is to give
copies of the papers, we have endeavored to follow
the orthography in all its variations and errors. In
this effort I am indebted to Mr. WM. G. MAZYCK,
by whom the proofs have been carefully compared
with the *original manuscript* as far as its partial
mutilation permitted. It may be proper to state
that the original publication was printed from a
copy made by myself with care before the manuscript had suffered mutilation.

The names with an *asterisk* (*) have the word
" Fridenizons " or " Fridenizé " in the margin of
the manuscript. Opposite the name of I. CAILLA-
BEUF, the note is " Fridenizé 2 fois."

These notes refer, no doubt, to grants of civil
privileges from the Lords Proprietors, or from the
King. One of the names with the asterisk is that
of the Rev. ELIAS PRIOLEAU. I am in possession
of a notarial certificate of " *Letters Patent of Den-*

zation" granted to him and his family on the 15th of April, in the third year of James II. It is dated " London, 25 April, 1687." As the document belongs to the history of the Colony at that period a copy is added in an appendix.

It does not appear that the list was presented to the General Assembly, but at its supposed date the Subject of Naturalization occupied largely the minds of the Colonists. Applications for Naturalization were before the General Assembly, as appears from the Naturalization Act of 10 March, 1696. It is probable that the provisions of that Act made the presentment of this List unnecessary. Having one of the Certificates of Naturalization issued by Governor Blake under that Act, I add a copy in the Appendix.

The names are not numbered in the manuscript List. The numbers have been added for the purpose of giving Alphabetical Indexes.

One more remark. From the entry opposite the first name on list No. 3, and the words "*passer gratis*," opposite another name on the same list, some expense probably attended the collection of the information required which was met by contributions.

Daniel Ravenel.

Charleston, September, 1867

[From the *City Gazette*, of Thursday, May 11, 1826.]

The following numbers were published in the *Southern Intelligencer* in 1822. The list of families given in the fourth number has enabled a descendant of one of them to trace out a branch of the family remaining in France. This circumstance has led to an agreeable reciprocation of civilities, and has increased the interest naturally attaching to so curious a document. In order to obtain for them a more extensive circulation, and that they may be more generally seen and perused by the decendants of the French refugees, these numbers are now published at the request of this gentleman

[From the *Southern Intelligencer*.]

THE FRENCH REFUGEES.

NO. I.

The invention of printing, and the early efforts of the Reformers, found the general mind fettered by ignorance and debased by superstition. While, however, its latent energies were roused by the one, the other contributed to its enlightenment, and a great moral revolution was their necessary consequence. But important changes in the moral, like those in the material world, are attended by those deep and convulsive throes by which Providence awakens the slumbering fears and affections of man. We are not then to be surprised at the eventful history of the revolution in religion and morals which began to exhibit itself at the time alluded to. The gleams of light but partially and imperfectly diffused afforded an unfavorable medium through which to view the feelings, the motives, and the objects of those who promoted the reformation. Where doubt exists of the tendency of new propositions, apprehension throws its weight into the scale, and determines us to the support of received opinions. Men of ordinary discernment could scarcely fail to see in the reformation an engine of too much power to be disregarded. The opinions of the Reformers were therefore in the sober judgement of many, and through the fears of more, dreaded as subversive of all the institutions of society ; while bigotry and interest, fanaticism, and superstition, magnified the evils of which the new-born spirit of the times was deemed the prolific parent. "An opinion prevailed, which had been zealously propagated by priests and implicitly received by sovereigns, that heresy was close-connected with rebellion, and that every great alteration in the church involved a like revolution in the civil government."

But opposition is the parent of zeal; persecution, of manly independence and perseverance. Efforts to counteract the new opinions contributed in general to their progress and influence : inquiry was excited, intellect roused, and an impatience of that thraldom to which mankind in general had been subjected became more and more apparent. The new opinions spread from town to town, from district to district, and from kingdom to kingdom, until their influence was felt throughout the whole civilized world.

France participated largely in the civil commotions of which the reformation was so prolific. The opinions of the Reformers had made their way into France, and had encountered persecution in the reign of Francis I., who came to the throne in 1515. Henry II., his son and successor, in 1559 issued an edict inflicting the penalty of death on dissenters, with an order to the judges " not to mitigate the punishment as had hitherto been the practice," and it is said to have been " a point of honor whether the one sect could exercise or the other suffer most barbarity."

On the death of Henry II. this violence was greatly moderated, yielding to the natural influence of the steadfast and virtuous course pursued by the champions of the new doctrines. But in the subsequent reign, that of Francis II. (the first husband of the celebrated " Queen of Scots "), the execution of the penal statutes was revived, and several distinguished personages headed the Protestant party, among them the King of Navarre, the Prince of Conde, and Admiral Coligni, who, at much personal risk, gave a respectability and character to the party, which contributed not a little to increase its numbers.

The first civil war between the Catholics and Huguenots took place in 1562, in the reign of Charles IX., and after a very sanguinary conflict at Dreux, a peace was concluded in terms favorable to the latter.

A few years afterwards, the Queen Regent concluded with Philip of Spain, " *the league of Bay-*

onne," the object of which was the *universal exter-mination of the Protestants by fire and sword.* Conde and Coligni, having obtained information of the league, resolved to strike the first blow ; and the battle of St. Dennis and the seige of Chartres produced an accommodation. In consequence, however, of a plan then formed to seize the prince and admiral, they escaped to Rochelle, and the war was renewed. In the battle of Yarnec, in 1569, Conde lost his life, and Coligni placed at the head of the Huguenots the young prince of Navarre (afterwards the celebrated Henry IV.). In this contest the fortune of war seemed against them, but such was the elastic spirit by which they were animated that, when Charles thought them almost annihilated, they presented themselves in formidable array in another quarter. Paris was threatened, and an accommodation concluded, by which liberty of conscience was allowed to the Hugonots.

This accommodation was the basis of one of the most detestable and disgraceful instances of perfidy and cruelty which history records. Charles seemed studious to show that he was sincere in the arrangement with the Huguenots. He punished all who infringed it, and proposed a marriage between his sister and Henry of Navarre. A few days after the marriage, when many of the nobility whom the solemnity had brought to Paris, were still there, a general massacre took place by order of the king,

who "himself (says Hume) in person led the way to
the assassinations. The hatred long entertained by
the Parisians against the Protestants, made them
second without any preparation the fury of the
court; and persons of every condition, age, and
sex, suspected of any propensity to that religion,
were involved in an undistinguished ruin." "The
streets of Paris flowed with blood, and the people,
more enraged than satiated with their cruelty, as if
repining that death had saved the victims from farther insult, exercised on their dead bodies all the
rage of the most licentious brutality. About 500
gentlemen and men of rank perished in the massacre, and near 10,000 of inferior condition. Orders
were instantly despatched to all the provinces for a
like general execution of the Protestants; and in
Rouen, Lyons, and many other cities, the people
emulated the fury of the capitol." Many of the
Protestants who lived near the frontier fled into
England, Germany, and Switzerland, while those
who lived in the interior escaped to the garrisons of
their party. The Huguenots, the victims of a base
and perfidious policy, though sad, were unsubdued.
They possessed at this time nearly one hundred
cities, castles, and fortresses, and in a short time
had an army of 18,000 men.

This massacre is called the massacre of St. Bar-
tholomew, as it took place on the feast of St. Bar-
tholomew, 24th August, 1572. Coligni, so long the

vigilant supporter of the cause of the Hugonots, fell a victim to this barbarous policy. Henry, prince of Conde, and Henry of Navarre were spared, but were obliged to recant their tenets.

In 1574 the war was renewed by Henry III. Henry of Navarre again joined the Huguenots, and strengthened their cause by the influence of his character and virtues. The Huguenots received an important accession of force from a German army under Conde, to the raising of which Elizabeth of England had contributed considerable sums. The fifth peace was concluded in 1576, and on better terms for the Huguenots than any former one. This peace, the result rather of the policy than the sincerity of Henry, produced great discontent among the Catholics, "The holy league" was now formed to prevent the increase of any other than the established mode of worship. France now exhibited the strange spectacle of a nation divided into three parties ; for, though the king was a member of the league, the Duke of Guise was its efficient head ; and strengthened by the powerful pretext of religion, it became formidable to the throne itself, and the very existence of the league was inconsistent with the terms of pacification made with the Hugonots. Thus the Royalists, the Leaguers, and the Protestants were armed against each other ; the first party headed by the king, the second by Henry, Duke of Guise, and the last by Henry, King of Navarre. This civil war has consequently been termed the war of the three Henries. On the death of the Duke of Anjou, in 1584, Henry of Navarre becoming heir presumptive to the throne, the league declared him incapable of the succession ; and their army having entered Paris, the king sanctioned this declaration. The king, however, perceiving that the throne was the great aim of the policy of the Duke of Guise, caused him and his brother to be assassinated; but this disgraceful act aroused the vengeance of the league against him, and a decree of the Sorbonne released his subjects from their allegiance. In this state of things, Henry III. joined the Protestant party, but soon afterwards, while beseiging Paris, he was assassinated by James Clement, a young Dominican friar, who, led on by fanaticism, at the risk and expense of his own life, entered the Protestant camp for the purpose. It has been said of Henry " that he spent his whole life in making war against the Protestants, and at last he was murdered by the Catholics."

Henry, King of Navarre, a Bourbon, was now the heir of the crown, but acknowledged by only a part of the nation. A war was conducted with various success, and Henry concluded at length to end it by what seemed the only means of obtaining a full recognition of his title—by the renunciation of the Protestant faith. He accordingly made a formal abjuration of it in the year 1593.

The Edict of Nantz, which guaranteed to the Protestants the full enjoyment of their faith and worship, the glory of this reign, was made in 1598. It was now upwards of eighty years since the bigotry of the times evincing its jealousy of the Protestant faith began to follow with bitter persecution those who embraced it ! For the first fifty years they groaned under hardships which it was probably imprudent to resist. General, open, and decided resistance, as we have seen, first took place in 1562, and from this time to the issuing of the edict of Nantz, a period of only thirty-six years, France had experienced no less than six civil wars, founded on differences in religious faith.

Although there must have been much of devoted attachment to the doctrines and establishments of religion to render the feeling connected with them so powerful an engine, we are not to attribute these civil wars to motives merely religious. Religion furnished a ready pretext to ambitious men, which bigotry rendered subservient to their views.

The period which elapsed from the passage of the Edict of Nantz to its final revocation was about eighty-seven years. But party spirit had excited too many prejudices and animosities on both sides, and the active efforts of the Hugonots had made them too secure to allow an empire under such circumstances to remain in uninterrupted peace. No very general serious disturbance took place till

1621, when the Hugonots, offended at the court, held a consultation at Rochelle, the result of which was a civil war of a year's duration, which ended in merely a confirmation of the Edict of Nantz. The professed object of this revolt was nothing less than to make France a republic, an object too serious and alarming in its nature to allow the government to remain satisfied, while a numerous party, discontented both from principle and habit, upon those subjects too by which the spirit of revolt was most easily roused, were so powerful at least for defence. The state of the party was inconsistent with enlightened policy, it being in many respects *imperium in imperio.* It was therefore one of the objects of the celebrated Richelieu, who became the minister of Louis XIII. in 1624, to reduce the power of the Hugonots. Rochelle was their stronghold. In 1627 this city was beseiged. But it being impossible to take it while the communication with the sea remained open, Richelieu constructed an immense mole across the harbor, a mile in length, and thus reduced the city to famine. After a fourteen months' seige it surrendered, on condition that the inhabitants should retain their property and the free exercise of their religion. The Cardinal had the fortifications demolished, after which the other fortified places successively yielded to the power of the government. Thus was the great object which first employed the powerful mind of this minister fully accomplished. The Protestants were no longer an independent and distinct people in the kingdom.

Louis XIV. was, like his predecessor, fortunate in having another Richelieu in Cardinal Mazarin, who maintained the tranquillity of the empire and increased the power of the monarch. He was also much indebted to the genius of Colbert, whose financial efforts multiplied the resources of the government. Under his care and patronage commerce and manufactures flourished. The Protestants, many of whom were engaged in manufactures, participated in his favor. But soon after the death of this great man, who so well understood the true happiness of his country, *Louis in 1865 revoked the Edict of Nantz*, and the horrors of persecution were again the disgrace and the scourge of France.

A Descendant of the Refugees.

[From the *City Gazette* of Friday, May 12th, 1826.]

From the Southern Intelligencer.

THE FRENCH REFUGEES.

NO. II.

The revocation of the edict of Nantz, obliged above half a million of Protestants to leave the dominions of Louis, and seek religious liberty in other countries.

Their hard fate could scarcely fail to excite the sympathy of all who were not the subjects of a blind bigotry, or indifferent to the happiness of their fellow-men.

In the reign of James II. considerable collections were made for the Refugees who went over to England; and in that of William, $15,000 were voted by Parliament, "to be distributed among persons of quality and all such as through age or infirmity were unable to support themselves." While encouragement was offered to artificers and manufacturers to settle in Great Britain, and to others to to migrate to America.[1]

South Carolina participated in the benefits which

[1] 1 Hewit's "History Carolina," 108.

25

the industry and moral habits of the people afforded to the countries in which they settled.

From a comparison of the names of the Refugees mentioned in Ramsay's "History of South Carolina," and those contained in the Act of Naturalization of 1696, with a very old manuscript list (which will be particularly noticed hereafter) we obtain the names of not less than 170 families and individuals who made this State their asylum, soon after the tyrannical and impolitic act, which induced them to emigrate.

A large proportion of the French settled on the south side of Santee River, where a town was laid out and called " Jamestown." This portion of country hence obtained the name of *French Santee*. Many settled in Charleston and its vicinity. There was also a settlement of them in the part of Berkley County, called the *Orange Quarter*, which was afterwards made the Parish of St. Dennis ; and about ten families were settled in St. Johns, Berkley.

All the accounts we have of the Refugees, represent them as a religious and moral people, making orderly, industrious, and valuable citizens.

The Refugees supposed, that in uniting their destinies with those of the English Colonists, they were securing to themselves the rights and privileges of citizens ; and it is probable that no circumstance occurred for the first year or two to make them doubt the correctness of that impression.

We may naturally conclude that the acquisition
of lands was among the inducements held out to
the French to come to the province. They generally purchased lands, and the circumstances of
some enabled them to obtain large tracts. They
took the oath of allegiance to the king and of fidel-
ity to the proprietors.[1] It is evident that the lords
proprietors wished them to be considered citizens,
for during the administration of Governor Ludwell
(about 1691), instructions were received from them,
by which he was required to allow them all the
rights and privileges of English settlers, and six
representatives in the assembly of the province.[2]

These instructions produced great discontent
among the English settlers. National antipathies
and prejudices are said to have been previously revived; much unpleasant feeling was now excited;
and the intentions of the proprietors opposed, upon
the ground that the Refugees were *foreigners*, and
under all the disabilities of *aliens*.

It was accordingly contended that the proprietors had no authority to allow them representatives
in assembly; that they were not entitled to vote at
elections; nor to the privilege of sitting as jurors:
that the titles by which they held their lands were
invalid; and that these disabilities could be removed
only by an act of naturalization. To these objec-
tions was added another, which as it was connected

---

[1] 1 Hewit, p. 10.   [2] 1 Hewit, p. 111;—1 Ramsay, p. 44.

with their religious tenets, was calculated to excite the feelings which had already borne so many wounds. It was said that the marriages performed by their ministers were unlawful, and that the children of such marriages were illegitimate.

These views, which affected so seriously the objects that are dearest to us on earth, produced considerable solicitude in the minds of the Refugees ; and after consultation amongst themselves they addressed the lords proprietors on their difficulties.

The lords proprietors instructed Governor Ludwell to inform them " that they would inquire what does in law qualify an alien born for the enjoyment of the rights and privileges of English subjects, and in due time let them know ; that for their part they would take no advantage of the present grievous circumstances of the Refugees ; that their lands should descend to such persons as they thought proper to bequeath them ; that the children of such as had been married in the same way, were not deemed bastards in England, nor could they be considered such in Carolina, where such unlimited toleration was allowed to all men by their charter " (1 *Hewit,* p. 113).

This favorable reply relieved their anxiety, but effected no change of sentiment in the English colonists. The Refugees were not allowed to choose a representative at the next election ; and the English settlers now addressed a remonstrance to the

Governor on the privileges claimed by them. Things remained in this state when Governor Archdale arrived from England, about 1694–'5. He was himself one of the proprietors, and had been specially deputed, at the suggestion of Landgrave Smith, to come to Carolina with full power to settle various matters of difficulty and discontent in the province. Among other matters, the concerns of the Refugees occupied his attention, but such was the state of public feeling, that he believed "their exclusion from all concerns in legislature absolutely necessary to the peaceable convocation of the delegates."

Lord Archdale belonged to the society of Friends. He is represented to have been a man of piety, humanity, and intelligence, highly respected and esteemed by the colonists. Although he remained in Carolina about eighteen months, and evinced a zealous interest in the welfare of the province, he was unable to overcome the jealousy existing between the English and French settlers. Yet it is remarkable that within a few months after his departure for England, an act was passed by the assembly, in March, 1696–'7, for their benefit, entitled *"An act for making aliens free of this part of the province,"* etc.[1]

This act was founded on an application for naturalization, made by the Refugees, by the advice of

[1] Trott's Laws, p. 61.

Governor Blake and some other friends.[1] We may infer from its adoption at this time that the disputes between the English and Refugees had other foundation and support than mere prejudice and national animosity. There is no doubt that these had long been exhibited to a considerable degree ; but they were most probably excited by honest differences of opinion respecting their constitutional rights. The *principle* involved in the claims of the Refugees appears to have been the great difficulty. It is reasonable to suppose that the one party were reluctant to ask for benefits to which they believed themselves entitled, and that a just regard to the rights of sovereignty prevented in the other an acquiescence in claims to which they deemed their sanction necessary.

This supposition is strengthened by a review of the act itself. It commences with a general clause for the naturalization of aliens, which is restrained by a proviso in the third section, " that no person whatsoever other than the persons therein expressly named, viz. (63 persons are here named), which have already petitioned the General Assembly for the liberties, privileges, and immunities aforesaid, shall have any benefit thereby, except such persons shall within three months next ensuing, petition in writing under their hands the Hon. Jos. Blake, Governor, etc., for the same." The fifth section, too,

---

[1] 1 Hewit, p. 139 ; 1 Ramsey, p. 51.

requires "that for the better manifestation and proof of their having petitioned," Governor Blake shall give to each petitioner a certificate of his having done so, and of having taken the oath prescribed.

There appears to have been four French congregations in this colony, viz.: at Santee, Charleston, Orange Quarter, and St. John's, Berkley. They professed the doctrines, and worshipped according to the forms of the Church of Geneva. But the distinctive features of three of these churches yielded to the arrangements made by the act of Assembly, called "*The Church Act*," passed in 1706.

By this act, all congregations and places of worship according to the usage of the Church of England, for the maintenance of whose minister, etc., any certain income or revenue is established by law, are declared settlers and established churches. It then incorporates certain parishes, placing the churches in them upon the same footing just described. Among them is "one in the Orange Quarter for the use of the French settlement there," called the parish of St. Dennis ; and another " in Craven County, in that part of it which is commonly known by the name of the French settlement on Santee River"; and the church built in Jamestown was made the parish church.

The incorporation of these two settlements appears to have been founded on an application made by them ; and their object must have been the support which their churches would derive from the government.

Mr. Humphreys, in his history of the Society for the Propagation of the Gospel in Foreign Parts, in speaking of the French settlement of *Orange Quarter*, says: " The major part of them usually met together in a small church, where they generally made a pretty full congregation when they had a minister among them : they were poor and unable to support their minister, and made an application to the Assembly of the province to be made a parish, and to have some public allowance for a minister Episcopally ordained, who should use the liturgy of the Church of England and preach to them in *French*." [1]

In speaking of the settlement at Santee, he says : " In the year 1706 they petitioned the Governor and Assembly to have their settlement erected into a parish," professing for the doctrines and discipline of the Church of England a high esteem.[2]

As most of the inhabitants of Orange Quarter and Santee were ignorant of the English language, the Church act, after reciting that fact, allows them, in conforming to usages of the Church of England, to use the Book of Common Prayer, translated into French by Dr. John Durell by order of Charles II., which had been approved by the Bishop of London.

[1] Humphrey's " Hist. Soc. for the Propagation of the Gospel in Foreign Parts," p. 105.   [2] Humph., p. 118.

The Rev. Mr. Philip De Richbourg was the first minister of the incorporated Church of St. James, Santee. He died in 1717, and it was not until 1720 that another was obtained. The Rev. Mr. Pouder-ous, a French clergyman, then took charge of the parish.[1]

The parish Church of St. Dennis was built about the year 1708,[2] and the Rev. Mr. Le Piere was the minister.[3]

It appears that St. Dennis was included within the bounds of St. Thomas' parish, and that its being made a separate parish was for the accommodation of the French inhabitants. It was, therefore, pro-vided by an act of Assembly in 1708 (founded, it would seem, on the fact of there being an admixture of English then among them) that whenever the services should be performed in English, the Church of St. Dennis should become a Chapel of Ease to the parish of St. Thomas (Trott's Laws, 155).

The small French congregation in St. John's, Berkley, appears soon to have been merged in the Episcopal Church. In 1707 the Rev. Mr. Maule, a missionary from the Society for the Propagation of the Gospel in Foreign Parts, took the charge of the parish. The English having no house of wor-ship (the parish church not having been commenced till 1710), he used often the small church of the

---

[1] Humph., p. 117.   [2] Humph., p. 105.
[3] Dalcho's "Ch. Hist.," p. 285.

French congregation, which the Rev. Mr. Tuillard, their minister, had offered ; and such of the French as understood English went to hear him.[1]

The French Calvinistic Church in Charleston only adhered to its peculiar worship, and this it continues to do at the present day. The church was built anterior to 1693.[2] It appears that the time of worship in this congregation was regulated by the tide, for the accommodation of such of them as came to town by water. The Governor and council having passed an order that they should meet for worship at the same hour as the other churches, they remonstrated against this exercise of authority, assigning to the lords proprietors as a reason for the custom they had adopted the accommodation of the members who lived out of the town. The proprietors directed that they should not be interfered with in this regulation.[3] This church at an early period acquired a property in some low lots, which, having increased in value, have long afforded an important revenue.

A Descendant of the Refugees.

[1] Humph., p. 88.   [2] Dalcho, p. 23.   [3] Dalcho, p. 29.

[From the *City Gazette*, of Saturday, May 13, 1826.]

From the Southern Intelligencer.

THE FRENCH REFUGEES.

NO. III.

In the year 1700 Mr. John Lawson visited the French settlement on Santee River, on a tour which he made through the interior of this State and North Carolina. In 1709 he published an account of his travels under the title of "A Journal of a Thousand Miles, Travelled Through Several Nations of the Indians, etc." This book is now a very scarce one. Judge James, in the introduction to his "Life of Marion," states that only two copies are known to be in the State. As this circumstance will be deemed a sufficient apology for using its contents freely, I have extracted so much of it as relates to the French settled on the Santee, to form the present number. A notice of them at that early period, however brief and cursory, will not be uninteresting to their posterity.

" The first place we designed for," says Mr. Lawson, " was Santee River, on which there is a

35

colony of French Protestants, allowed and encouraged by the lords proprietors."—p. 7.

Having given a minute account of his voyage from Charleston through the inland passage to Santee, which occupied a week, he adds: "As we rowed up the river we found the land towards the mouth, and for about sixteen miles up it, scarce any thing but swamp and percoarson, affording vast cyprus trees, of which the French make canoes that will carry fifty or sixty barrels. After the tree is moulded and dug they saw them in two pieces, and so put a plank between, and a small keel, to preserve them from the oyster banks, which are innumerable in the creeks and bays betwixt the French settlement and Charleston. They carry two masts and Bermuda sails, which makes them very handy and fit for their purpose ; for although their river fetches its first rise from the mountains, and continues a current some hundreds of miles ere it disgorges itself, having no sound, bay, or sand banks betwixt the mouth thereof and the ocean, notwithstanding all this, with the vast stream it affords at all seasons, and the repeated freshets it so often alarms the inhabitants with, by laying under water great part of their country, yet the mouth is barred, affording not above four or five foot water at the entrance."—p. 9.

This is a pretty accurate description of the large cypress canoes which are in such general use at the

present day—and it is probable that the French
at Santee were the first people in the State who
built them.

" There being a strong current in Santee River,
caused us to make a small way with our oars.
With hard rowing, we got that night to Mons.
Eugee's [Huger] house which stands about fifteen
miles up the river, being the first Christian dwelling
we met withal in that settlement, and were very
courteously received by him and his wife."

" Many of the French follow a trade with the
Indians, living very conveniently for that interest.
There is about seventy families seated on this
river, who live as decently and happily as any
planters in these southward parts of America.
The French being a temperate, industrious people,
some of them bringing very little of effects, yet by
their endeavors and mutual assistance amongst
themselves (which is highly to be commended),
have outstripped our English, who brought with
them larger fortunes, though as it seems less en-
deavor to manage their talent to the best advantage."

" We lay all that night at Mons. Eugee's, and
the next morning set out farther, to go the remainder of our voyage by land."—" At noon we
came up with several French plantations, meeting
with several creeks by the way, the French were
very officious in assisting with their small dories to

pass over these waters (whom we met coming from
their church), being all of them clean and decent in
their apparel ; their houses and plantations suitable
in neatness and contrivance.   They are all of the
same opinion with the Church of Geneva, there
being no difference amongst them concerning the
punctilios of their Christian faith ; which union hath
propagated a happy and delightful concord in all
other matters throughout the whole neighborhood ;
living amongst themselves as one tribe or kindred,
every one making it his business to be assistant to
the wants of his countryman, preserving his estate
and reputation with the same exactness and concern
as he does his own ; all seeming to share in the
misfortunes, and rejoice at the advance, and rise, of
their brethren."

"Towards the afternoon we came to Mons.
L'Jandro [Gendron], where we got our dinner;
there coming some French ladies whilst we were
there, who were lately come from England, and
Mons. L'Grand, a worthy Norman, who hath been
a great sufferer in his estate by the persecution in
France, against those of the Protestant religion.
This gentleman very kindly invited us to make our
stay with him all night, but we being intended
farther that day, took our leaves, returning ac-
knowledgements of their favors."

"About four in the afternoon we passed over a
large cypress run in a small canoe. The French

doctor sent his negro to guide us over the head of a large swamp, so we got that night to Mons. Galliar's [Gaillard] the elder, who lives in a very curious contrived house, built of brick and stone, which is gotten near that place. Near here comes in the road from Charlestown, and the rest of the English settlement, it being a very good way by land, and not above thirty-six miles, although more than one hundred by water; and I think the most difficult way I ever saw, occasioned by reason of the multitude of creeks lying along the main, keeping their course through the marshes, turning and winding like a labyrinth, having the tide of ebb and flood twenty times in less than three leagues' going."

He then describes a freshet in the Santee, representing the adjacent "woods to seem like some great lake, except here and there a knoll of high land, which appeared above the water."

"We intended for Mons. Galliar's, Jr., but were lost, none of us knowing the way at that time, although the Indian was born in that country, it having received so strange a metamorphosis."

"When we got to the house we found our comrades" [who had been accidentally separated from them] "and several of the French inhabitants with them, who treated us very courteously, wondering at our undertaking such a voyage, through a country inhabited by none but savages, and them of so different nations and tongues."

"After we had refreshed ourselves, we parted from a very kind, loving, and affable people, who wished us a safe and prosperous voyage,"—pp. 12 to 15.

A DESCENDANT OF THE REFUGEES.

[From the *City Gazette*, of Monday, May 15, 1826.]

From the Southern Intelligencer.

THE FRENCH REFUGEES.

NO. IV.

The paper of which the subjoined *List* is a copy has been deemed worthy of publication, on account both of its matter and its antiquity. As a document relating to the early history of our State, it is interesting: and may perhaps be useful. The descendants of many of the persons included in it will doubtless be gratified by an opportunity of possessing a copy in print, and particularly those to whom it will afford information respecting their ancestors, of which, from the want or the loss of family records, they have been ignorant.

It was discovered in a parcel of old papers which belonged to *Henry De St. Julien*, of St. John's, Berkley, who died in that parish at about seventy years of age, in 1768 or 9, and who was the youngest son of Pierre De St. Julien, whose name is included in the list. His papers passed into the hands of a sister who survived all the family, and died at an advanced age in the year 1780.

The present possessor of the paper is one of her lineal descendants.

We can scarcely doubt that this compilation was intended to accompany an application for naturalization. The caption by which it purports to be *a list of French and Swiss Refugees who wished to be naturalized;* the fulness and minuteness of its details; and the unpleasant differences between the French and English settlers on the subject of citizenship, noticed in the second of these numbers—all lead to this conclusion.

The following considerations render it probable that it was prepared with a view to the provisions of the act of naturalization of 1696.

It will be recollected that this act confers the rights and privileges of citizens on sixty-three persons, who petitioned the general assembly, and who are specially named therein; and that it then provides that all the benefits of the act should be extended to such other persons as should petition therefor within three months, requiring that "for the further manifestation and proof of their having petitioned," Governor Blake should give to each a certificate of his having done so, of having complied with the other requisites of the act, and of being consequently entitled to the privileges conferred by it. The writer of these remarks has in his possession one of the certificates of Governor Blake, issued in conformity with this act and referring to it by its date and title. It is the certificate of citizenship of *one of the refugees on this list*, and bears date the 3d of June, 1697.

There are two circumstances, however, which show that it must have been prepared before the passage of the act of 1696, though they do not affect the conclusion with respect to its object. The one is, that several of the persons included in it are made citizens by name in the act of 1696; the other, that upon consulting the family Bible of one of the individuals on the list, now in the possession of a descendant in this city, it appears that a child whose name is given in the list was born in May, 1694, and died in September, 1695—the inference from which circumstance is that the paper was prepared, *or its materials collected*, between these dates.

It is believed that no complete list of the French Refugees has ever been published; probably none has been compiled. This list, with that in Ramsay's "History of South Carolina," and that in the act of 1696, will probably afford the names of most, if not all, of the class of settlers who made this State their asylum immediately after the revocation of the Edict of Nantz.

I will only add that the two persons first named on the list were clergymen, viz.: Elias Prioleau and L. P. Trouillart, the latter being, no doubt, the pastor of the small French congregation in

St. John's, Berkley, noticed in the second of these numbers.

A DESCENDANT OF THE REFUGEES.

LISTE

Des François et Suisses Refugiez en Caroline qui souhaittent d'être naturalizés Anglois.

1. * ELIAS PRIOLEAU, fils de Samuel Prioleau et
    de Jeanne Merlat, né à   en Xain-
    tonge en France.
    Jeanne Burgeaud, sa femme, né en L'isle de Ré.
    Jeanne, leur fille, née à St. Jean D' Angely.
    Samuel, Marie, et Ester, leurs enfans néz en
    Caroline.

2. LAURENT PHILIPPE TROUILLART, né à la fette
    Regnault Roidam, fils de Pierre Trouillart
    et de Marie.
    Madeleine Maslet, sa femme née á cet.
    Élizabet et Madeleine leurs filles néz en Caro-
    line.

3. JACQUES BOYD.
    Jean Boyd, Gabriel Boyd, frères néz à Bour-
    deaux, et fils de Jean Boyd et de Jeanne.
    Jeanne Berchaud, femme du dit Jean Boyd.
    Jeanne Élizabet Boyd, Jacques Boyd, Jean

Auguste Boyd, enfans du dit Jean Boyd, et de la dite Jeanne Berchaud, néz en Caroline.

4. *Paul Bruneau de Riuedoux, Escuyer, fils de Arnaud Bruneau, et de   né à la Rochelle.

Henri Bruneau, est fils de Henri Bruneau, et de Marie, né à la Rochelle.

5. Jacques Le Serurier, né à St. Quantin en Picardie fils de Jacques Le Serurier, et de Marie Le Comte.

Élizabet Leger, sa femme.

6. *Pierre De St. Julien, Malacare, né à Vitre en Bretagne, fils de Pierre St. Julien, Malacare, et de Jeanne Le Febure.

Damaris Élizabet Le Serurier, sa femme.

Pierre et Jacques, leurs enfans, néz en Caroline.

7. Abraham Fleury, De la Pleine, né à Tours, fils de Charles Fleury, et de Madeleine Soupzmain.

Marianne Fleury, sa fille, veuve de Jacques Dugué, née à Paris, et Marianne Dugué, fille du défunct Jacques Dugué, et du dit arianne Fleury, née en Caroline.

8. *Daniel Hugur, né à Loudun, fils de Jean Huger, et Anne Rassin.

Margueritte Perdriau, sa femme.

Margueritte Huger, leur fille, née à Rochelle.

Daniel et Madeleine Huger, leurs enfans, néz en Caroline.

9. *ISAAC CAILLABEUF, né à Ste. Soline, fils de Louis Caillabeuf et de Marie Charuyer.
    Rachel, Fanton, sa femme.
    Isaac, Etienne et Anne Caillabeuf, leurs enfans, néz en Caroline.

10. PIERRE LA SALLE, né à Bourdeaux, fils de Charles La Salle, et de Susanne Hugla.
    Élizabeth Messett, sa femme.
    Pierre et Élizabeth La Salle, leurs enfans néz en Caroline.

11. FRANÇOIS DE ROUSSERIE, né à Montpelier, fils d'Alexandre DeRousserye, et de Marie Suranne.

12. PIERRE BURETEL, né à la Rochelle, fils de Charles Buretel, et de Sara Bouhier.
    Élizabeth Chintrie, sa femme.

13. DANIEL BONNEL,   fils de Jean Bonnel, et de Marie Lalon.
    Marie Izambert, sa femme.
    Susanne Bonnel, leur fille, née en Caroline.

14. JONAS BONHOSTE, né à Paris, fils de Pierre Bonhoste et de Marie Garlin.
    Catherine Allaire, sa femme.
    Jonas Bonhoste, leur fils né en Caroline.

15. PIERRE DUGUÉ, Isaac Dugué, son frère, et Élizabeth Dugué, leur sœur, néz à Bésance en Bery, enfans de Jacques Dugué et d'Élizabet Dupuy.

16. JACQUES DU BOSC, né à St. Ambroise en

Languedoc, fils d' André Du Bosc, et de Marie Le Stoade.

Marie Dugué, sa femme.

Marie Du Bosc, leur fille née en Caroline.

17. PHILIPE NORMAND, né à Germain en Poitou, fils de Philipe Normand, et de Jeanne Pineau.

Élizabet Juin, sa femme.

18. ANTHOINE BONNEAU, né à la Rochelle, fils de Jean Bonneau et de Catherine Roi.

Catherine Du Bliss, sa femme.

Anthoine Bonneau, Jean Henri Bonneau, leurs enfans néz en France, et Jacob Bonneau, leur fils né en Caroline.

19. PIERRE COLLIN, né en L'isle de Ré, fils de Jean Collin, et de Judith Vasleau.

20. PIERRE POINSET, l' aîné, né à Soubize, fils de Pierre Poinset, et Marie sa femme.

21. PIERRE POINSET, le jeune, né à Soubize, fils du dit Pierre et Sara Fouchereau.

Anne Gobard, sa femme.

22. PIERRE BACOT, né à Tours, fils de Pierre Bacot et de Jeanne Moreau.

Jacquine Mercier, sa femme.

Pierre et Daniel Bacot, frères, leurs fils, néz en France, et Élizabeth Bacot, leur fille, née en Caroline.

23. NOÉ ROYER, l' aîné, né à Tours, fils de Sébastien Royer et de Marie Rendon.

Madeleine Saulnier, sa femme.

Pierre Royer, et Madeleine et Marie Royer, leurs enfans, néz en France.

24. Noé Royer, le jeune, né à Tours, fils de Noé Royer, et de Madeleine Saulnier.

Judith Giton, sa femme.

25. Jacques Nicholas, petit Bois, né à Chalais en Xaintonge, fils de Daniel Nicholas, et de Léonore Gast.

26. Pierre Le Chevallier, né à St. Lo en Normandie, fils de Roland Le Chevallier et d'Ester Dallain.

Madeleine Garillon, sa femme.

27. Paul Pepin, né à Grenoble, fils d'Alexandre Pepin, et de Madeleine Garillon.

28. Mathurin Guérin, né à St. Nazaire, et Xaintonge, fils de Pierre Guérin, et de Jeanne Billebaud.

Marie Nicollas, sa femme.

29. Jacques Gallopin, né à Laigle en Normandie, fils de Siméon Gallopin, et de Louise Malherbe.

30. Charles Fromaget, né à Chatelerault, fils de Charles Fromaget et de Marie Le Nain.

31. Noé Seré, né à Luminie en Brie, fils de Claude Seré, et d'Ester Gilliet.

Catherine Challiou, sa femme.

Noé Seré, et Margueritte Seré, leurs enfans, néz en Caroline.

32. JEAN LEBERT, né à Redon en Bretagne, fils de Pierre Lebert, et de Jeanne Guernier.

33. ISAAC BATON, né à Leschelle en Picardie, fils de Corneille Baton et de Judith Voyenne.

Jacques Baton, né à Londre, et Isaac Baton, né en Caroline, fils du dit Baton, et de Marie De Lorme.

34. DANIEL JOUET, né à L'isle de Ré, fils de Daniel Jouet, et d'Élizabeth Jouet.

Marie Courcier, sa femme.

Daniel et Pierre Jouet, leurs enfans, néz en France.

Marie Jouet, leur fille, née à Plymouth, Élizabeth et Annie Jouet, aussi leur filles néz à Niew York.

35. LOUIS THIBOU, né à Orléans, fils de Jean Thibou, et de Marie Callard.

Charlotte Mariette, sa femme.

Louis Thibou, Charlotte Thibou, néz en Paris.

Jacob Thibou, Louise Thibou, néz en Caroline.

Gabrielle Thibou, née à Londres.

Isaac Thibou, née à la Nouvelle-Yorck.

36. FRANÇÓISE MOUNART, née à Chainé en Poitou, fille de Jacques Mounart, et d' Anne Bonneau.

Jacques Marseau, né à Chainé en Poitou, fils de Gabriel Marseau, et de Françoise Mounart.

37. GABRIEL RIBOUTEAU, né à Lachaume, en Poitou, fils d' Éstienne Ribouteau, et de Catherine Girardot.

38. *JACQUES DE BOURDEAUX, né à Grénoble, fils de Evremond De Bourdeaux et de Catherine Fresné.

    Madeleine Garillond, [?] sa femme.

    Madeleine Judith, leurs filles néz à Grenoble.

    Anthoine, Jacques, Israel, De Bourdeaux, leurs enfans néz en Caroline.

39. JEAN GIRARDEAU, né à Tattemont en Poitou, fils de Pierre Girardeau et de Catherine Lareine.

40. ÉSTIENNE TAUVRON, né à L'isle de Ré, fils de Jacques Tauvron et de Marie Brigeaud.

    Madeleine Tauvron, sa fille, née à L' isle de Ré.

    Ester Tauvron, née à Plymouth.

41. JACQUES LARDAN, né à Dieppe, fils de Jacques Lardan et de Marie Poulart.

    Marthe Moreau, sa femme.

    Jacques Lardan, leur fils né en Caroline.

42. JEAN HERAUD, né à Oleron, fils de Heraud et de

43. MARIE TAUVRON, née à l' Isle de Ré, fille de Jacques Tauvron et de Marie Brigeaud.

    Moyse Le Breun, né à l' Isle de Ré, fils de Moyse Le Breun et de la ditte Marie Tauvron.

44. ISAAC MAZICQ, natif de l'Isle de Ré, fils de Paul Mazicq, et de Hélesabeth Vanewick.
   Marianne Le Serrurier, sa femme.
   Marie Anne Mazicq, leur fille, née en Caroline.

45. ANNE VIGNAUD, née au Porte des Barques en Xaintonge, veuve de Charles Faucheraud.
   Anne Faucheraud, et Gedson Faucheraud, néz au Porte des Barques, enfans du dit Charles Faucheraud et de Anne Vignaud.
   Marie Faucheraud, leur fille née en Angleterre.

46. JEAN THOMAS, né à St. Jean D'Angely en St. Onge, fils de Jean Thomas et d'Anne Dupon.

47. DANIEL DUROUZEAUX, né à St. Jean D'Angely, fils de Daniel Durouzeaux, et Marye Souchard.
   Élizabeth Foucheraud, sa femme.
   Daniel, Pierre, leurs enfans, néz en Caroline.

48. *LOUIS PASQUERAU, né à Tours, fils de Louis Pasquerau et de Madeleine Chardon.

49. AUGUSTE MEMIN, né à la Forge Nosśay en Poitou, fils de Jean Memin et de Marye Masiot.

50. ABRAHAM LESUEUR, né de Harfleur en Normandie, fils d'Isaac Lesueur et de Marye Senee.
   Catherinne Poinsett, sa femme.

51. ÉLIZABETH GARNIER, veuve de Daniel Horry,

fille de Daniel Garnier et de Elizabeth
Fanton, nativé de l'Isle de Ré.

Élizabeth Marye, Lidie, Marye, filles de Daniel
Horry, et de la ditte Élizabeth Garnier, néez
en Caroline.

52. ANTHOINE BOUREAU, né à Lusinain en Poitou,
fils de Jean Boureau et de Marguerite
Gourdain.

Jeanne Braud, sa femme.

Jeanne Boureau, leur fille n e en Angleterre.

53. HENRY PERONNEAU, né à la Rochelle, fils de
Samuel Peronneau et de Jeanne Collin.

54. ANTHOINE CORDES, né à Bazamet en Langue-
doe, fils de Paul Cordes et de Marie De-
peuch.

Ester Madeleine Balluet, sa femme.

Isaac, Madeleine, Ester, leurs enfans, néz en
Caroline.

55. PIERRE GIRRARD, né à Poitiers, fils de Pierre
Girrard et de Judith Fruschard.

56. SUZANNE HORRY, née à Neu Chatell en Suize
veuve de Jacques Varin, fille de Samuel
Horry et de Jeanne Dubois.

Suzanne, Jacob, leurs enfans, néz en Caroline.

57. SAMUEL DU BOURDIEU, Escuyer, né à Vitré
en Bretagne fils d' Olivier Du Bourdieu et
de Marie Genne.

Judith Dugué, sa femme.

Louis Philipe Du Bourdieu, fils du dit Samuel

Du Bourdieu et de Louise Thoury, né en
Caroline.

Samuel Du Bourdieu, fils du susdit et de la
ditte Judith Dugué, né en Caroline.

58. ÉLLYE BISSET, né à St. Jean D'Angely, fils
d'Abraham Bisset et de Marye Bitheur.

Jeanne Poinset, sa femme.

Anne, Catherinne Bisset, leur filles néez en
Caroline.

59. JEAN PECONTAL, né à Cossade en Languedoc,
fils de Jean Pecontal, et d'Anne Nonnelle.

60. JÉRÉMIE COTHONNEAU, né à la Rochelle, fils de
Germain Cothonneau et d'Élizabeth Nom-
bret.

Marye Billon, sa femme.

Germain Pierre, leurs enfans, néz à la Rochelle.

Ester Marthe, leur fille, née en Caroline.

Liste des habitants de Santee.

61. FRANÇOIS DE ROUSSERYE, né à Montpellier,
fils de   De Rousserye et de

62. PIERRE GAILLARD, né à Cherneux en Poitou,
fils de Pierre Gaillard et de Jacquete
Jolain.

Élizabeth Leclair, sa femme.

Cleremonde, leur fille, née en Caroline.

Élizabet et Marthe Melet, nées à la Nouvelle

Yoorck, filles de Jean Melet et de la ditte Leclair.

63. *Jean François Gignilliat, né à Venay en Suise, fils d'Abraham Gignilliat et de Marye de Ville.

Suzanne Le Serrurier, sa femme.

Marye Élizabeth, Henry, Pierre, Abraham, leurs enfans néz en Caroline.

64. Mr. Jacques Le Bas, né à Can, fils de Jean Le Bas et Anne Samborne.

Pierre Le Bas, son fils, né à Can, sa mère Catherine Varing, faut éscrire à Mes. M : et S: pour scavoir le nom de ses père et mère.

65. Marie Fougeraut, veuve de Moyse Brigaud.

66. Pierre Couillandeau, né à la Tramblade, fils de Pre. Couillandeau et de Marie Fougeraut.

67. Jean Potell, né à Diepe, fils de Nicholas Potell et de Marye Brugnet.

Madeleine Pepin, sa femme.

Jean, Pierre, Jacques, Jean, leurs enfans, nez en Caroline.

68. Marye Brugnet, née à Diepe, veuve de Nicholas Potell.

69. *Jean Gendron, } frères, fils de David
70. *Philippe Gendron, } Gendron, et Caterine Gendron, sa femme, néz à Maran, province d'Onis.

Magdelaine Gendron, femme du dit Philippe
Gendron, fille de Chardon et de
Chardon à Tours en Tourenne.

Jean, Magdelaine, Élizabeth, Mariane, Jeane
Gendron, fils et filles de Phillippe Gendron
et de Magdelaine Gendron, ci-devant femme
de Louis Pasquereau, néz en Caroline.

————, Pierre, Isaac, Charles, Pasquereau,
fils de défunt Louis Pasquereau, et Magde-
leine Pasquereau sa femme, les trois pre-
miers néz à Tours, et Charles né à Londre.

71. PIERRE GUERRI, fils de Jaques Guerri, et
d'Anne Guerri, de Seuvet en Poitou, et

Jeanne Guerri, sa femme, fille de Louis Broussard et de Judith Broussard, du dit lieu.

François, né à Dublin, Jean, Pierre, Jean
Jaques, Jeane Élizabeth Guerri, enfans du
dit Pierre Guerri, et d'Anne Guerri, néz en
Caroline.

72. ISAAC DUBOSC, fils de Louis Dubosc et d'Anne
Dubosc, de Dieppe en Normandie,

Suzanne Dubosc, sa femme, fille de Pierre
Couillandeau, et de Susane Couillandeau,
native de la Tramblade en Xaintonge.

73. JEAN GUIBAL, fils de Henry Guibal et de
Claude Guibal, de St. André de Val
en Languedoc.

Ester Guibal, sa femme, fille de Jean le Cert,
et Marie le Cert de Rennes en Bretagne.

74 JOACHIM GAILLARD, fils de Jean Gaillard et
    Marie Gaillard, de Montpellier en Langue-
    doc.

Ester Gaillard, sa femme, fille d'André Paparel
    et Caterine Paparel, de Bouin en Forest.

Jean, Pierre Gaillard, enfans du susdits Joakim
    Gaillard et Ester Gaillard,

75. JAQUES BOYD,   ⎫ fils de défunt Jean Boid et
76. JEAN BOYD,   ⎬ de Jeanne Boyd, de Bor-
77. GABRIEL BOYD,   ⎭ deaux province de Guienne.

Jeane Boyd femme de Jean Boyd, fille de
    Élie Berchaud et Jeanne Berchaud de la
    Rochelle : province d'Onis.

Jeanne, Élizabeth, Jacques, Jean Auguste, en-
    fans, de Jean, et de Jean ne Boyd, nézen
    Caroline.

78. PIERRE ROBERT, M: D: St. E: fils de Daniel
    Robert, et Marie Robert de St. Imier en
    Suisse.

Jeane Robert, fille de Jean Bayer et Susane
    Bayer, de Bale en Suisse.

Pierre Robert, fils du dit Pierre Robert et de
    Jeane Robert, natif de Bale en Suisse.

79. * PAUL BRUNEAU, de Revidoux, Écuyer, fils de
    défunt Arnaud Bruneau de la Chabossiere,
    Écuyer, et de   de la Chabossiere,
    natif de la Rochelle, province d'Onis.

80. * HENRY BRUNEAU, fils de défunt Henry Bru-
    neau de la Chabossiere, Écuyer, et de Marie

de la Chabossiere, né à la Rochelle, province d'Onis.

81. ANDRÉ REMBERT, fils de François Rembert, et de Judith Rembert, de Pont en Royan en Daufiné.

Anne Rembert, sa femme, fille de Jean et Loüise Bressan, du dit lieu.

Anne, André, Gerosme, Pierre Susane, Jeane Rembert, enfans des susdits, néz en Caroline.

82. RENÉ RAVENEL, fils de Daniel Ravenel et de Marie Ravenel, de Vitré en Bretagne.

Charlotte Ravenel, fille de   De St. Julien de Malacare, née à Vitré en Bretagne.

Jeanne Charlotte, Daniel, René Ravenel, enfans des susdits, néz en Caroline.

83. * HENRY AUGUSTE CHATAGNER, Écuyer, } fils
84. * ALEXANDRE THÉSÉE CHATAGNER,

de défunt Roch Chatagner, Écuyer, et de Jeanne de Chatagner, néz à la Rochelle : province d'Onis.

Élizabeth Chatagner, femme du susdit Alexandre Thésée Chatagner, fille de Pierre Buretel et d'Elizabeth Buretel.

Alexandre Chatagner, Élizabeth Madeleine Chatagner, enfans des susdits, néz en Caroline.

85. DANIEL SENESCHAUD, fils de Jonas Seneschaud, et de Jeane Seneschaud, de St. Maixant en Poitou.

Magdelaine Seneschaud, sa femme, fille de
Daniel Ardouin et de Marie Ardouin, de
Gémoset en Xaintonge.

Élizabeth Seneschaud, fille des susdits néz en
Caroline.

86. ISAAC LE GRAND, Écuyer, fils de Jean Le
Grand Sr. d'Anvuile, et de Marie Le Grand,
natif de Caen en Normandie.

Élizabeth Le Grand, femme du dit Sr. Le
Grand, fille de Jean Dieu et de Judith Dieu,
de Caen en Normandie.

Isaac Le Grand, leur fils né en Caen idem.

Élizabeth Le Grand, leur fille, née en Caroline.

87. PIERRE MANIGAUD, }
88. GABRIEL MANIGAUD, } frères, fils de Gabriel
Manigaud et de Marie Manigaud, natifs de
la Rochelle païs d'Onis.

89. PIERRE MICHAUD, fils de Jean Michaud, et de
Caterine Michaud, de la Viledieu d'Onai,
province de Poitou.

Sarra Michaud, sa femme, fille de Jacques
Bertomeau, et Élizabet Bertomeau, née en
l'Isle de Ré, ci-devant femme de Élie Jodon.

Abraham Michaud, frère du susdit Pierre
Michaud : idem, et

Ester Michaud, sa femme, fille d'Élie Jodon,
et Sara Jodon, née en l'Isle de Ré.

Jeane, Ester, Charlotte Michaud, leurs enfans,
néz en Caroline.

Daniel Jodan, fils d'Élie Jodon et Sara Jodon, né en l'Isle de Ré.

90. JEAN PIERRE PELÉ, fils de Pierre Pelé et Judith Pelé, natif du Païs de Vaud en Suisse, et Gabrielle Pelé, sa femme.

91. JEAN PROU, fils de Moyse Prou et de Sara Prou, né en Poitou.

Jeane, Jean, Charlotte Prou, ses enfans et de défunte Jeane Prou.

92. NICHOLAS LE NUD, fils de Nicholas, et Marie Le Nud, de Dieppe, en Normandie.

93. DANIEL LE GENDRE, fils de Jacques Le Gendre et de Maurice   de Rouen en Normandie.

94. ÉTIENE TAMPIÉ, fils de   Tampié et de

95. LOUIS DUTARQUE, né en Picardie, fils de Mathias Dutarque, et de Anne Foulon.

96. ANTHOINE POITEUM, né à Maintenon, fils d'Anthoine Poiteum et de Garielle Berou.

Margueritte De Bordeaux, sa femme.

97. GEORGE JUING, né à Cherneux en Poitou, fils de René Juing et de Judith Pié.

Suzanne Le Riche, sa femme, née à Londre.

Jean Juing, leur fils né en Caroline.

98. NICHOLAS BOCHET, né à Nanteuil les maux [?] en Brye, fils de Nicholas Bochet et de Marguerite Petit.

Suzanne Dehays, sa femme.

Suzanne, leur fille, née en France.

Pierre et Nicholas, néz en Caroline.

99. ABEL BOCHET, frère du dit Nicholas Bochet, né au dit lieu de Nanteuil.

100. *PIERRE VIDEAUL, né à la Rochelle, fils de Pierre Videaul, et de Madelaine Burgaud.
Janne Élizabeth, sa femme.
Janne Élizabeth, leur fille, née à Londre.
Pierre Nicholas, leur fils, Marianne Videaul, Marthe Ester Videaul, Judith Videaul, Janne Videaul, et Madelaine Videaul, nés en Caroline.

101 JACQUES BENOIT, fils de Jacques Benoit et de Gabrielle Mercier, né à Sussay en Poitou.
Jean Benoit, son fils né en France.
Sara Mounié, femme du dit Jacques Benoit.
Jacques et Pierre néz en Caroline.

102. ISAAC FLEURY, né à Tours, fils de Charles Fleury et de Medalaine Soubmain.

103. FRANÇOIS GUERRIAN, fils de Pierre Guerrian et de Janne Billebeau, né à St. Nazere en Saintonge.
Anne Arriné, sa femme.

104. JEAN BOISSEAU, né à Maraine, fils de Jacques Boisseau et de Marie La Court.
Marie Postel, sa femme.

105. JEAN BERTEAUD, né à St. Lo, fils de Jean Berteaud et de Marguerite Robert.

106. ÉLLYE HORRY, né à Charenton, fils de Jean Horry et de Madelaine Du Fréne.

107. ISAAC PORCHER, né à St. Severe en Berry, fils
d'Isaac Porcher, et de Suzanne Ferre.
Claude Cheriny, sa femme.
Isaac, Pierre, Élizabeth, Madelaine, et Claude,
leurs enfans, néz en Angleterre, et en
Caroline.

108. CLAUDE CARRON, né à Tours, fils de Michel
Carron et de Élizabeth Belong.

109. PIERRE MOUNIER, né en l'Isle de Ré, fils de
Louis Mounier et d' Élizabeth Martineaux.
Louise Robinet, sa femme.

110. NICHOLAS DE LONGEMARE, l' aîné, né à la
Forêt de Lyone, en Normandie, fils de
Jacques de Longemare et d'Adrienne
Aracheguene.

111. NICHOLAS DE LONGEMARE, né à Diepe, fils
du dit Longemare et d'Anne Le Roy.
Marie Bonneau, sa femme.

112. JEAN CARRIÈRE, né en Normandie, fils de Jean
Carrière.

113. LOUIS GOURDAIN, né à Concourt en Artois,
fils de Valentin Gourdain et de Marye
Piedeuin.

114. BENJAMIN MARION, né à la Chaumé en Poitou,
fils de Jean Marion et de Périnne Bou-
tignon.
Judith Baluet, sa femme.
Ester, Gabrielle, et Benjamin, leurs enfans,
néz en Caroline.

115. DANIEL GARNIER, né en l'Isle de Ré, fils de Daniel Garnier et de Marie Chevallier.

Élizabeth Fanton, sa femme.

Étienne Garnier, Rachel Garnier, Margueritte Garnier, Anne Garnier, leurs enfans néz en l'Isle de Ré.

116. LOUIS DE ST. JULIEN, né à Vitré, fils de Pierre St. Julien et de Jeanne Le Febure.

117. HONORÉ MICHAUD, né à la Tour de Pé, en Suisse, fils de Jean Michaud et de

118. MOISE CARION, né à Faugère en Languedoc, fils d'André Carion et de Marie Fascal.

Anne Ribouteau, sa femme.

Moise Carion, leur fils.

119. ÉSTIENNE TAMPLÉ, né en Xaintonge, fils de Éstienne Tamplé, et de Jeanne Prinseaud.

Marie Du Bosc, sa femme.

☞ NO. 2.

Liste des Noms des Fransioise qui se recuille en l' Églize du Cartie d' Orange.

120. premièrement, ANTHOINE POITEUIN, natif d' Orsemont province de Gaule en France, fils de Jacque Poiteuin et Jenne Modemen, et de Gabrielle Bérou sa femme, native d' Ormey en Bause, fille d' Utrope Bérou et d'Andrée Le Prou.

121. DANIEL TREZEVANT, fils de Théodore Treze-
vent et de Susanne Menou, natif d'Authon
en Perche, et Susanne Maulard sa famme,
native de Chanseuille en Bause, province
en France, fillie de Lubin Maulard et de
Gabrielle Berou.

122. PIERRE DUTARTRE, fils de Daniel Dutartre et
d'Anne Rénault, natif de Chathaudun en
Bause, province de France, et Anne Poiteuin sa famme, native de Duplesis Morné,
province de Gaule en France, fille d'Anthoinne Poiteuin et de Gabrielle Bérou.

123. ANTHOINE POIDEUIN fils, natif de Menthenon, province de Gaule en France, fils
d'Anthoinne Poideuin et de Gabrielle
Bérou, et de sa famme Marguerite De
Bourdos, native de Grenoble en Dofiné,
province de France, fillie de Jacque De
Bourdos et de Madelenne Garilian.

124. PIERRE POITEUIN, natif de Menthenon, province de Gaule en France, fils d'Anthoinne
Poiteuin et de Gabrielle Bérou.

125. JOSEPH MARBEUF, natif de Vielle Vigne en
Bretagne, fils de Julien Marbeuff et d'Ester
Robin.

126. JEAN AUNAUT, natif de Nisme, fils de Jean
Aunant et de Sibelle Dumas, et de famme
Marie Soyer, native de Diepe en Nor-
mandie.

127. SOLOMON BREMAR, natif d'Anseme en Picardie en France, fils de Jacque Bremar et de Marthe Le Grande, et sa famme Marie Sauvagot, native d'Alleurs, pais Saintonge en France, fille de Jean Sauvagot et de Madelenne Potet.

128. NICHOLAS BOUCHET, natif de Nantheil les meaux, Susanne Deshais sa famme, native de Magny poroisse de Boutigny, Susaune, sa fillie native de Fublainne, province de Brie en France.

129. DANIEL TREZEVANT, fils de Daniel Trezevant et de Susanne Maulard, natif de Menthenon, province de Gaule en France.

Monsieur : à l'égar des noms que je n'écri pas, ce sont les suivants. Lesquels ne démeure pas au Cartie ;

LOUIS PICAR, LOUIS GOUDIN.

Lesquels sont à la Pointe, vous poure les éscrire vous mesme. Il lui en na ausi que je pas mis, lesquels vous trouverre éscrit au Commité, comme Mr. Vidot et quelquautre.

☞ NO. 3.

Liste des François et Suisses.

130. Made. BACOT,   donné cinquante chelin.
131. Mons. PIERRE BACOT, natif de tours, fils de Pierre Bacot et Jeanne Moreau. Jacquine

Mercier, fille d'Alncham Mercier et Jac-
quine Sélipeaux. Pierre Bacot leur fils et
Daniel Bacot, natif de Tours, et Élizabet
Bacot, leur fille, natit en Carolinne.

132. NOÉL ROYER de Tours, fils de Sébastien
Royer et Marie Rendons, ses père et mère
demeurant à Tours, et Madelainne Saunier,
sa femme, natit de Chateleraulx, fille de
Jacques Saunier et Judith Baudon ses père
et mère. Pierre Royer, Madelinne Royer
et Marie Royer, leurs enfans néz à Tours.
Noél Royer, natif de Tours, fils de Noél
Royer et Madelainne Saunier. Judith
Giton, sa femme, native de la Voulte en
Dauphinée, fille de   Giton et de
        Cottin, ses père et mère.

133. JACQUES NICHOLAS, dit petit Bois, natif de
Chalais en Xaintonge, fils de Daniel Nicholas, et Léonor Gast, ses père et mère,

134. PIERRE LA CHEVALIER, natif de St. Lo en
Normandie, fils de Rolland le Chevallier et
d'Ester Dallain, ses père et mère, et Madelainne Garillion, sa femme, natit de Grenoble, fille d'Israel Garillion et Susanne
Saunier, sa mère.

135. PAUL PEPIN, natit de Grenoble, fils d'Alexandre Pepin et de Madelainne Garillon.

136. MATHURIN GUÉRIN, natif de St. Nazaire, en
Xaintonge, fils de Pierre Guérin, et de

Jeanne Bilbau, et Marie Nicholas, sa femme, natit de la Chaumé en Poitou, fille d'André Nicholas et de Françoise Dunot.

137. JACQUES GALLOPIN, natif de Laigle en Normandie, fils de Siméon Gallopin, et de Louise Malherbe.

138. CHARLES FROMAGET, natif de Chateleraulx, fils de Charles Fromaget et de Marie Lenain.

139. NOÉL SERRÉ, natit de Luminie en Brye, fils de Claude Serré, et d'Ester Gilliet, et Catherinne Challion, sa femme, native de Lyon, fille de Louis Challion et de Benoite Pitauer, et Margueritte Serré, et Noél Serré, leurs enfans, natits en Caroline.

140. PIERRE COULANDAUX, natif de la Tremblade, fils de Pierre Coulandaux, et de Marie Fougerout.

141. MARIE FOUGEROUT, veuve de Moise Brigaud ; elle natit de la Tremblade.

142. ISAAC BATON, né à l'Echelle en Trèvache, fils de Cornille Batton et de Judith Voienne, et Isaac Batton, son fils né en Carollinne, et Jacques Batton, son fils né à Londre. Leur mère est morte elle s'appelloit Marye de Lorme, natif de Vadenouste.

143. PIERRE MOUNIER, natit de l'isle de Rée, fils de Louis Mounier et d'Élizabeth Martinaux, et Louise Robinet sa femme, fille de Louis

Robinet, et elle ne sayt pas le nom de sa mère.

144. NICHOLAS DE LONGUEMARE, natît de la fôret de Lyone en Normandie, fils de Jacques de Longuemore et d'Adrienne Archeguenne. Nicolas de Longuemare, fils du dit Nicholas de Longuemare et d'Anne le Roy, ses père et mère. Il est natit à Dieppe.

145. LOUIS DU TARQUE, natit à   en Picardie, fils de Mathieu du Tarque et d'Anne

146. JACQUES LE SERURIER, natit en   fils de Pierre le Serurier et de Marie le Coure, et Élizabeth Le Ger sa femme, native du dit lieu, fille de Jacques Le Ger et d'Élizabeth Bossu.

147. ÉLYE HORRY, natif de Charenton, fils de Gehan Horry et de Madelainne du Frenne.

148. DANIEL JOUET, fils de Daniel Jouet et d'Élizabeth Jouet, natif de l'Isle de Rée, et Marie Coursier sa femme, fille de Gehan Coursier et de Anne Perrotau, et Daniel, Pierre Jouet leurs enfans, tous de l'Isle de Rée, et Marie Jouet leur fille née à Plimouth, et Élizabeth et Anne Jouet nées à Nouville Yorck.

149. FLORENT PHILIPPE TROULLIARD, natif de la Fetté Regnault, ditte le vidame, fils de défunct Pierre Troüillard, vivant professeur

en Théologie, et de Marie Troüillard. Madeleine Masset femme du dit Fl. Ph. Troüillard, Élizabet et Madeleine Troüillard, leurs filles nées en Caroline.

150. ALARD BELAIN.

151. CARION.

152. PORELL.

153. Mr. LONGEMARE le père.

154. JEAN DOUCET.

APPENDIX.

A Certificate of the Denization of Elias Prioleau, his Wife and Children.

I, Nicholas Hayward, Notary & Tabellion Public dwelling in *London*, admitted & sworn, do hereby certify and attest unto all whom it may concern, That I have seen & perused certain Letters Patents of Denization, granted by our Soveraign Lord King *JAMES* the Second, under the Broad Seal of *England*, dated the Fifteenth day of April, in the Third year of his said Majesties Reign ; Wherein, amongst others, is inserted the Names of Elias Prioleau, Clerk, Jane his wife, Elias and Jane their children, who, though born beyond seas, are made His Majesties Liege Subjects, and to us held, reported, and taken as subjects born in this Kingdom of *England ;* and may, as such, purchase, buy, sell and dispose of Lands, Tenements, and Heredi- taments in this Kingdom, or any other of his Majes- ties dominions, as freely peaceably & entirely as any subject born in this Kingdom ; and that the said Elias Prioleau, Clerk, Jane his Wife, Elias and Jane their Children, by Virtue of the said Letters Patents, are to pay Custom and Duties for their

Goods and Merchandise only as Natives do and ought to do and to enjoy all Liberties, Privileges and Franchises of Subjects born in this Kingdom, without any disturbance, impediment or molestation, as by the said Patent, relation being thereunto had, may more at large appear. Of all which, Act being required of me, the said Notary, I have granted these Presents to serve and avail the said Elias Prioleau, Clerk, Jane his Wife, Elias and Jane their Children, in time & place convenient.

London, the 25th day of Aprill Anno Dom. 1687.

In Testimonium Veritatis, signo meo Manuali solito sigavi & Tabelliona-
[SEAL.]   *tus mei Sigillum apposui rogatus.*

NIC⁰. HAYWARD, No. Pub.

Cert' Naturalization, Elias Prioleau, Minister of y' Gospel. 1697 Carolina.

The Rᵗ Honᵇˡᵉ JOSEPH BLAKE, Esqʳ One of the true & absolute Lords
[SEAL.]   and Proprietors of Carolina, Commander in Chief, Vice-Admiral and Governor Genˡ of South Carolina.

To all Judges, Justices, Magistrates, Ministers and Officers Ecclesiastical and Civil and to all persons whatsoever, to whom this shall come to be seen, heard, read or known, Greeting.

Know ye that Elias Prioleau, Minister of ye Gospel, and Janne his daughter, born under the allegiance of the King of France, hath taken the Oath of allegiance to our most Royal Sovereign William the Third, over England, Scotland, France, and Ireland King, Defender of the faith, and hath done every other thing which by Act of Assembly made at Charlestown, in the ninth year of the Reign of our Sovereign Lord King William, Anno Dom. One Thousand Six hundred & Ninety Six and Seven, entitled An Act to make Aliens free of this part of this Province and for giving Liberty of Conscience to all Protestants, he was required to do, and fully & effectualy, to all intents, constructions & purposes qualified and capacitated to have, use and enjoy all the privileges, Powers and Immunity of any person born in the Kingdom of England, to certify which I have hereunto sett my hand and fixed the public Seal of the province att Charlestown this Third day of June Anno 1697,

JOSEPH BLAKE.

Recorded in the Secretary's Office, June the 4th 1697, p^r me

JA. MOORE,
Secretary.

INDEX NO. 1.

INDEX NO. 2.

Female Heads of Families by their Maiden Names.

75

FINIS.

www.ingramcontent.com/pod-product-compliance
Lightning Source LLC
Chambersburg PA
CBHW070518090426
42735CB00012B/2831